Wilson Language Basics

Composition Book

Level 3

Wilson works.

FIRST EDITION

Wilson Language Training Corporation

www.wilsonlanguage.com

www.fundations.com

Fundations® Student Composition Book 3

Item # STCBK3

ISBN 978-1-56778-275-2

FIRST EDITION

PUBLISHED BY:

Wilson Language Training Corporation
47 Old Webster Road
Oxford, MA 01540
United States of America

(800) 899-8454

www.wilsonlanguage.com

Printed in the U.S.A.

November 2007

1 Sit *right*

Seat pulled in, feet on floor

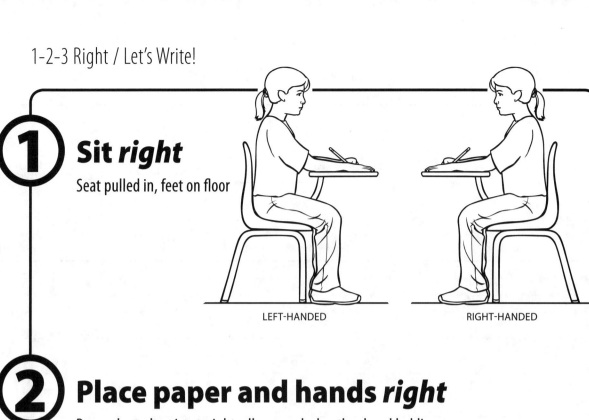

LEFT-HANDED RIGHT-HANDED

2 Place paper and hands *right*

Paper slanted, wrist straight, elbow on desk, other hand holding paper

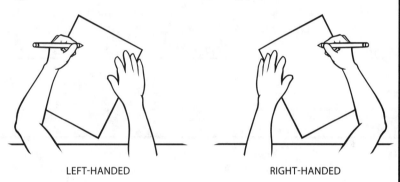

LEFT-HANDED RIGHT-HANDED

3 Grip pencil *right*

Pencil held between index finger and thumb, resting on the other fingers

LEFT-HANDED RIGHT-HANDED

 # Let's *write!*

Today's Date: _____ *Check-up* ☐

Sounds

1   2   3   4

Review Words

1   2

3   4

Current Words

1   2

3   4

Sound Alike Words

1   2

Review Trick Words

1   2

Sentences

1

2

Today's Date: _____ *Check-up* ☐

Sounds

1   2   3   4

Review Words

1   2

3   4

Current Words

1   2

3   4

Sound Alike Words

1   2

Review Trick Words

1   2

Sentences

1

2

Sounds

1   2   3   4

Review Words

1   2

3   4

Current Words

1   2

3   4

Sound Alike Words

1   2

Review Trick Words

1   2

Sentences

1

2

Sounds

1   2   3   4

Review Words

1   2

3   4

Current Words

1   2

3   4

Sound Alike Words

1   2

Review Trick Words

1   2

Sentences

1

2

Sounds

1   2   3   4

Review Words

1   2

3   4

Current Words

1   2

3   4

Sound Alike Words

1   2

Review Trick Words

1   2

Sentences

1

2

Sounds

1   2   3   4

Review Words

1   2

3   4

Current Words

1   2

3   4

Sound Alike Words

1   2

Review Trick Words

1   2

Sentences

1

2

Sounds

1   2   3   4

Review Words

1   2

3   4

Current Words

1   2

3   4

Sound Alike Words

1   2

Review Trick Words

1   2

Sentences

1

2

Sounds

1   2   3   4

Review Words

1   2

3   4

Current Words

1   2

3   4

Sound Alike Words

1   2

Review Trick Words

1   2

Sentences

1

2

Today's Date: _____ *Check-up* ☐

Sounds

1   2   3   4

Review Words

1   2

3   4

Current Words

1   2

3   4

Sound Alike Words

1   2

Review Trick Words

1   2

Sentences

1

2

Sounds

1   2   3   4

Review Words

1   2

3   4

Current Words

1   2

3   4

Sound Alike Words

1   2

Review Trick Words

1   2

Sentences

1

2

Sounds

1   2   3   4

Review Words

1   2

3   4

Current Words

1   2

3   4

Sound Alike Words

1   2

Review Trick Words

1   2

Sentences

1

2

Today's Date: _____ *Check-up* ☐

Sounds

1   2   3   4

Review Words

1   2

3   4

Current Words

1   2

3   4

Sound Alike Words

1   2

Review Trick Words

1   2

Sentences

1

2

Sounds

1   2   3   4

Review Words

1   2

3   4

Current Words

1   2

3   4

Sound Alike Words

1   2

Review Trick Words

1   2

Sentences

1

2

Sounds

1   2   3   4

Review Words

1   2

3   4

Current Words

1   2

3   4

Sound Alike Words

1   2

Review Trick Words

1   2

Sentences

1

2

Sounds

1   2   3   4

Review Words

1   2

3   4

Current Words

1   2

3   4

Sound Alike Words

1   2

Review Trick Words

1   2

Sentences

1

2

Today's Date: _____ *Check-up* ☐

Sounds

1   2   3   4

Review Words

1   2

3   4

Current Words

1   2

3   4

Sound Alike Words

1   2

Review Trick Words

1   2

Sentences

1

2

Sounds

1   2   3   4

Review Words

1   2

3   4

Current Words

1   2

3   4

Sound Alike Words

1   2

Review Trick Words

1   2

Sentences

1

2

Sounds

1   2   3   4

Review Words

1   2

3   4

Current Words

1   2

3   4

Sound Alike Words

1   2

Review Trick Words

1   2

Sentences

1

2

Today's Date: _____ *Check-up* ☐

Sounds

1   2   3   4

Review Words

1   2

3   4

Current Words

1   2

3   4

Sound Alike Words

1   2

Review Trick Words

1   2

Sentences

1

2

Sounds

1   2   3   4

Review Words

1   2

3   4

Current Words

1   2

3   4

Sound Alike Words

1   2

Review Trick Words

1   2

Sentences

1

2

Today's Date: _____ *Check-up* ☐

Sounds

1 _____ 2 _____ 3 _____ 4 _____

Review Words

1 _____ 2 _____

3 _____ 4 _____

Current Words

1 _____ 2 _____

3 _____ 4 _____

Sound Alike Words

1 _____ 2 _____

Review Trick Words

1 _____ 2 _____

Sentences

1 _____

_____

2 _____

_____

Sounds

1   2   3   4

Review Words

1   2

3   4

Current Words

1   2

3   4

Sound Alike Words

1   2

Review Trick Words

1   2

Sentences

1

2

Sounds

1   2   3   4

Review Words

1   2

3   4

Current Words

1   2

3   4

Sound Alike Words

1   2

Review Trick Words

1   2

Sentences

1

2

Sounds

1   2   3   4

Review Words

1   2

3   4

Current Words

1   2

3   4

Sound Alike Words

1   2

Review Trick Words

1   2

Sentences

1

2

Sounds

1 _____ 2 _____ 3 _____ 4 _____

Review Words

1 _____ 2 _____

3 _____ 4 _____

Current Words

1 _____ 2 _____

3 _____ 4 _____

Sound Alike Words

1 _____ 2 _____

Review Trick Words

1 _____ 2 _____

Sentences

1 _____

_____

2 _____

_____

Sounds

1   2   3   4

Review Words

1   2

3   4

Current Words

1   2

3   4

Sound Alike Words

1   2

Review Trick Words

1   2

Sentences

1

2

Today's Date: _____ *Check-up* ☐

Sounds

1 _____ 2 _____ 3 _____ 4 _____

Review Words

1 _____ 2 _____

3 _____ 4 _____

Current Words

1 _____ 2 _____

3 _____ 4 _____

Sound Alike Words

1 _____ 2 _____

Review Trick Words

1 _____ 2 _____

Sentences

1 _____

2 _____

Sounds

1   2   3   4

Review Words

1   2

3   4

Current Words

1   2

3   4

Sound Alike Words

1   2

Review Trick Words

1   2

Sentences

1

2

Today's Date: _____   *Check-up* ☐

Sounds

1   2   3   4

Review Words

1   2

3   4

Current Words

1   2

3   4

Sound Alike Words

1   2

Review Trick Words

1   2

Sentences

1

2

Sounds

1   2   3   4

Review Words

1   2

3   4

Current Words

1   2

3   4

Sound Alike Words

1   2

Review Trick Words

1   2

Sentences

1

2

Today's Date: _____ *Check-up* ☐

Sounds

1   2   3   4

Review Words

1   2

3   4

Current Words

1   2

3   4

Sound Alike Words

1   2

Review Trick Words

1   2

Sentences

1

2

Sounds

1   2   3   4

Review Words

1   2

3   4

Current Words

1   2

3   4

Sound Alike Words

1   2

Review Trick Words

1   2

Sentences

1

2

Today's Date: _____   *Check-up* ☐

Sounds
_____

1 _____ 2 _____ 3 _____ 4 _____
_____

Review Words
_____

1 _____ 2 _____
_____

3 _____ 4 _____
_____

Current Words
_____

1 _____ 2 _____
_____

3 _____ 4 _____
_____

Sound Alike Words
_____

1 _____ 2 _____
_____

Review Trick Words
_____

1 _____ 2 _____
_____

Sentences
_____

1 _____
_____

_____

2 _____
_____

Sounds

1   2   3   4

Review Words

1   2

3   4

Current Words

1   2

3   4

Sound Alike Words

1   2

Review Trick Words

1   2

Sentences

1

2

Today's Date: _____   *Check-up* ☐

Sounds

1 _____ 2 _____ 3 _____ 4 _____

Review Words

1 _____ 2 _____

3 _____ 4 _____

Current Words

1 _____ 2 _____

3 _____ 4 _____

Sound Alike Words

1 _____ 2 _____

Review Trick Words

1 _____ 2 _____

Sentences

1 _____

2 _____

Sounds

1   2   3   4

Review Words

1   2

3   4

Current Words

1   2

3   4

Sound Alike Words

1   2

Review Trick Words

1   2

Sentences

1

2

Sounds

1 _____ 2 _____ 3 _____ 4 _____

Review Words

1 _____ 2 _____

3 _____ 4 _____

Current Words

1 _____ 2 _____

3 _____ 4 _____

Sound Alike Words

1 _____ 2 _____

Review Trick Words

1 _____ 2 _____

Sentences

1 _____

_____

2 _____

_____

Sounds

1   2   3   4

Review Words

1   2

3   4

Current Words

1   2

3   4

Sound Alike Words

1   2

Review Trick Words

1   2

Sentences

1

2

Today's Date: _____ *Check-up* ☐

Sounds

1   2   3   4

Review Words

1   2

3   4

Current Words

1   2

3   4

Sound Alike Words

1   2

Review Trick Words

1   2

Sentences

1

2

Sounds

1   2   3   4

Review Words

1   2

3   4

Current Words

1   2

3   4

Sound Alike Words

1   2

Review Trick Words

1   2

Sentences

1

2

Sounds

1   2   3   4

Review Words

1   2

3   4

Current Words

1   2

3   4

Sound Alike Words

1   2

Review Trick Words

1   2

Sentences

1

2

Sounds

1 _____ 2 _____ 3 _____ 4 _____

Review Words

1 _____ 2 _____

3 _____ 4 _____

Current Words

1 _____ 2 _____

3 _____ 4 _____

Sound Alike Words

1 _____ 2 _____

Review Trick Words

1 _____ 2 _____

Sentences

1 _____

_____

2 _____

_____

Sounds

1 _____ 2 _____ 3 _____ 4 _____

Review Words

1 _____ 2 _____

3 _____ 4 _____

Current Words

1 _____ 2 _____

3 _____ 4 _____

Sound Alike Words

1 _____ 2 _____

Review Trick Words

1 _____ 2 _____

Sentences

1 _____

_____

2 _____

_____

Sounds

1   2   3   4

Review Words

1   2

3   4

Current Words

1   2

3   4

Sound Alike Words

1   2

Review Trick Words

1   2

Sentences

1

2

Today's Date: _____ _Check-up_ ☐

Sounds

1   2   3   4

Review Words

1   2

3   4

Current Words

1   2

3   4

Sound Alike Words

1   2

Review Trick Words

1   2

Sentences

1

2

Sounds

1   2   3   4

Review Words

1   2

3   4

Current Words

1   2

3   4

Sound Alike Words

1   2

Review Trick Words

1   2

Sentences

1

2

Today's Date: _____

Check-up ☐

Sounds

1   2   3   4

Review Words

1   2

3   4

Current Words

1   2

3   4

Sound Alike Words

1   2

Review Trick Words

1   2

Sentences

1

2

Wilson Fundations | ©2005 Wilson Language Training Corporation

Sounds

1 _____ 2 _____ 3 _____ 4 _____

Review Words

1 _____ 2 _____

3 _____ 4 _____

Current Words

1 _____ 2 _____

3 _____ 4 _____

Sound Alike Words

1 _____ 2 _____

Review Trick Words

1 _____ 2 _____

Sentences

1 _____

_____

2 _____

_____

Today's Date: _____ *Check-up* ☐

Sounds

1   2   3   4

Review Words

1   2

3   4

Current Words

1   2

3   4

Sound Alike Words

1   2

Review Trick Words

1   2

Sentences

1

2

Sounds

1   2   3   4

Review Words

1   2

3   4

Current Words

1   2

3   4

Sound Alike Words

1   2

Review Trick Words

1   2

Sentences

1

2

Sounds

1   2   3   4

Review Words

1   2

3   4

Current Words

1   2

3   4

Sound Alike Words

1   2

Review Trick Words

1   2

Sentences

1

2

Today's Date: _____ *Check-up* ☐

Sounds

1   2   3   4

Review Words

1   2

3   4

Current Words

1   2

3   4

Sound Alike Words

1   2

Review Trick Words

1   2

Sentences

1

2

Sounds

1   2   3   4

Review Words

1   2

3   4

Current Words

1   2

3   4

Sound Alike Words

1   2

Review Trick Words

1   2

Sentences

1

2

Today's Date:

Check-up ☐

Sounds

1   2   3   4

Review Words

1   2

3   4

Current Words

1   2

3   4

Sound Alike Words

1   2

Review Trick Words

1   2

Sentences

1

2

Sounds

1   2   3   4

Review Words

1   2

3   4

Current Words

1   2

3   4

Sound Alike Words

1   2

Review Trick Words

1   2

Sentences

1

2

Sounds

1 _____ 2 _____ 3 _____ 4 _____

Review Words

1 _____ 2 _____

3 _____ 4 _____

Current Words

1 _____ 2 _____

3 _____ 4 _____

Sound Alike Words

1 _____ 2 _____

Review Trick Words

1 _____ 2 _____

Sentences

1 _____

_____

2 _____

_____

Today's Date: _____ *Check-up* ☐

Sounds

1 _____ 2 _____ 3 _____ 4 _____

Review Words

1 _____ 2 _____

3 _____ 4 _____

Current Words

1 _____ 2 _____

3 _____ 4 _____

Sound Alike Words

1 _____ 2 _____

Review Trick Words

1 _____ 2 _____

Sentences

1 _____

2 _____

Sounds

1   2   3   4

Review Words

1   2

3   4

Current Words

1   2

3   4

Sound Alike Words

1   2

Review Trick Words

1   2

Sentences

1

2

Sounds

1   2   3   4

Review Words

1   2

3   4

Current Words

1   2

3   4

Sound Alike Words

1   2

Review Trick Words

1   2

Sentences

1

2

Sounds

1 — — — — — — 2 — — — — — 3 — — — — — 4 — — — — —

Review Words

1 _____ 2 _____

3 _____ 4 _____

Current Words

1 _____ 2 _____

3 _____ 4 _____

Sound Alike Words

1 — — — — — — 2 — — — — — —

Review Trick Words

1 — — — — — — 2 — — — — — —

Sentences

1 _____

_____

2 _____

_____

Today's Date: _____ *Check-up* ☐

Sounds

1   2   3   4

Review Words

1   2

3   4

Current Words

1   2

3   4

Sound Alike Words

1   2

Review Trick Words

1   2

Sentences

1

2

Sounds

1   2   3   4

Review Words

1   2

3   4

Current Words

1   2

3   4

Sound Alike Words

1   2

Review Trick Words

1   2

Sentences

1

2

Sounds

1   2   3   4

Review Words

1   2

3   4

Current Words

1   2

3   4

Sound Alike Words

1   2

Review Trick Words

1   2

Sentences

1

2

Sounds

1   2   3   4

Review Words

1   2

3   4

Current Words

1   2

3   4

Sound Alike Words

1   2

Review Trick Words

1   2

Sentences

1

2

Sounds

1   2   3   4

Review Words

1   2

3   4

Current Words

1   2

3   4

Sound Alike Words

1   2

Review Trick Words

1   2

Sentences

1

2

Sounds

1   2   3   4

Review Words

1   2

3   4

Current Words

1   2

3   4

Sound Alike Words

1   2

Review Trick Words

1   2

Sentences

1

2

Sounds

1   2   3   4

Review Words

1   2

3   4

Current Words

1   2

3   4

Sound Alike Words

1   2

Review Trick Words

1   2

Sentences

1

2

Sounds

1   2   3   4

Review Words

1   2

3   4

Current Words

1   2

3   4

Sound Alike Words

1   2

Review Trick Words

1   2

Sentences

1

2

Today's Date: _____ *Check-up* ☐

Sounds

1 ——— 2 ——— 3 ——— 4

Review Words

1 ——— 2

3 ——— 4

Current Words

1 ——— 2

3 ——— 4

Sound Alike Words

1 ——— 2

Review Trick Words

1 ——— 2

Sentences

1

2

Sounds

1   2   3   4

Review Words

1   2

3   4

Current Words

1   2

3   4

Sound Alike Words

1   2

Review Trick Words

1   2

Sentences

1

2

Sounds

1 _____ 2 _____ 3 _____ 4 _____

Review Words

1 _____ 2 _____

3 _____ 4 _____

Current Words

1 _____ 2 _____

3 _____ 4 _____

Sound Alike Words

1 _____ 2 _____

Review Trick Words

1 _____ 2 _____

Sentences

1 _____

_____

2 _____

_____

Sounds

1   2   3   4

Review Words

1   2

3   4

Current Words

1   2

3   4

Sound Alike Words

1   2

Review Trick Words

1   2

Sentences

1

2

Sounds

1   2

3   4

Sound Alike Words

1   2

3   4

Trick Words

1   2

3   4

Words

1   2

3   4

5   6

7   8

9   10

Sentences

1

2

Sounds

1   2

3   4

Sound Alike Words

1   2

3   4

Trick Words

1   2

3   4

Words

1   2

3   4

5   6

7   8

9   10

Sentences

1

2

Sounds

1 _____   2 _____

3 _____   4 _____

Sound Alike Words

1 _____   2 _____

3 _____   4 _____

Trick Words

1 _____   2 _____

3 _____   4 _____

Words

1 _____   2 _____

3 _____   4 _____

5 _____   6 _____

7 _____   8 _____

9 _____   10 _____

Sentences

1

2

Sounds

1 _____ 2 _____

3 _____ 4 _____

Sound Alike Words

1 _____ 2 _____

3 _____ 4 _____

Trick Words

1 _____ 2 _____

3 _____ 4 _____

Words

1 _____ 2 _____

3 _____ 4 _____

5 _____ 6 _____

7 _____ 8 _____

9 _____ 10 _____

Sentences

1

2

Sounds

1 _____ 2 _____

3 _____ 4 _____

Sound Alike Words

1 _____ 2 _____

3 _____ 4 _____

Trick Words

1 _____ 2 _____

3 _____ 4 _____

Words

1 _____ 2 _____

3 _____ 4 _____

5 _____ 6 _____

7 _____ 8 _____

9 _____ 10 _____

Sentences

1

2

Sounds

1   2

3   4

Sound Alike Words

1   2

3   4

Trick Words

1   2

3   4

Words

1   2

3   4

5   6

7   8

9   10

Sentences

1

2

Sounds

1   2

3   4

Sound Alike Words

1   2

3   4

Trick Words

1   2

3   4

Words

1   2

3   4

5   6

7   8

9   10

Sentences

1

2

Sounds

1   2

3   4

Sound Alike Words

1   2

3   4

Trick Words

1   2

3   4

Words

1   2

3   4

5   6

7   8

9   10

Sentences

1

2

Sounds

1 _____ 2 _____

3 _____ 4 _____

Sound Alike Words

1 _____ 2 _____

3 _____ 4 _____

Trick Words

1 _____ 2 _____

3 _____ 4 _____

Words

1 _____ 2 _____

3 _____ 4 _____

5 _____ 6 _____

7 _____ 8 _____

9 _____ 10 _____

Sentences

1

2

Sounds

1   2

3   4

Sound Alike Words

1   2

3   4

Trick Words

1   2

3   4

Words

1   2

3   4

5   6

7   8

9   10

Sentences

1

2

Sounds

1 _____   2 _____

3 _____   4 _____

Sound Alike Words

1 _____   2 _____

3 _____   4 _____

Trick Words

1 _____   2 _____

3 _____   4 _____

Words

1 _____   2 _____

3 _____   4 _____

5 _____   6 _____

7 _____   8 _____

9 _____   10 _____

Sentences

1

2

Sounds

1   2

3   4

Sound Alike Words

1   2

3   4

Trick Words

1   2

3   4

Words

1   2

3   4

5   6

7   8

9   10

Sentences

1

2

Sounds

1   2

3   4

Sound Alike Words

1   2

3   4

Trick Words

1   2

3   4

Words

1   2

3   4

5   6

7   8

9   10

Sentences

1

2

Sounds

1   2

3   4

Sound Alike Words

1   2

3   4

Trick Words

1   2

3   4

Words

1   2

3   4

5   6

7   8

9   10

Sentences

1

2

Cursive Letter Formation Groups | Lower Case

Forward Slant

a b c d e f

g h i j k l

m n o p q r s

t u v w x y z

Backward Slant

a b c d e f

g h i j k l

m n o p q r s

t u v w x y z

Wilson Fundations | ©2005 Wilson Language Training Corporation